MW00478177

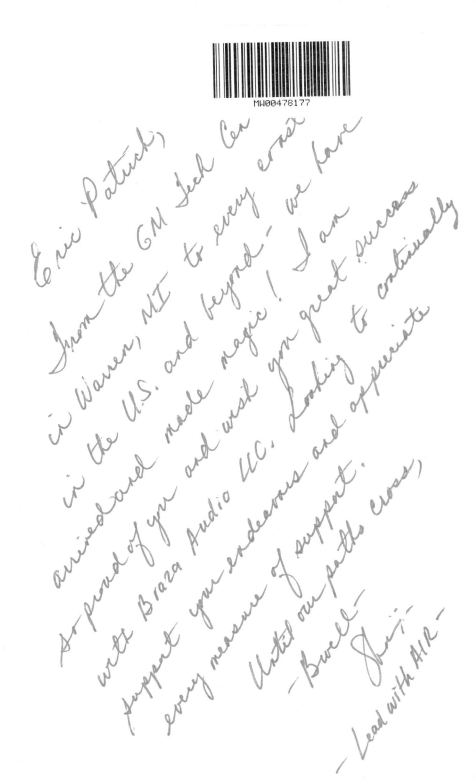

Eric Patrick,
from the GM Tech Cen
in Warren, MI to every coast
in the U.S. and beyond - we have
arrived and made magic! I am
so proud of you and wish you great success
with Braza Audio LLC. Looking to continually
support your endeavors and appreciate
every measure of support.
Until our paths cross,
-Bwell-
Sheri..
- Lead with AIR -

LEADERSHIP
—— IS ABOUT ——
BEHAVIOR, NOT TITLES

INSIGHTFUL TRAITS FOR ACTION, IMPACT, AND RESULTS

SHON BARNWELL
CHIEF MASTER SERGEANT, US AIR FORCE, RETIRED

Foreword by:
Chief Master Sergeant M. Lou Wetzel, US Air Force, Retired

BARNWELL
PUBLISHING

Barnwell Publishing LLC.,
1114 State Hwy 96, Suite C-1 #367, Kathleen, GA 31047

Barnwell, Shon
    Leadership Is about Behavior, Not Titles: Insightful traits for action,
    impact, and results

Copyright ©2020 by Shon Barnwell. All rights reserved. Printed in the
United States of America.

No part of this book may be reproduced or transmitted in any form or by
any means, electronic or mechanical, including photocopying, recording,
or by any information storage and retrieval system, without permission of
the Author or Publisher, except where permitted by law. Requests for permission should be addressed to Barnwell Publishing, Permissions, 1114
State Hwy 96, Suite C-1 #367, Kathleen, GA 31047; or online at
www.BarnwellPublishing.com.

Identifiers:
Paperback ISBN: 978-1-7356930-0-2
Hardback ISBN: 978-1-7356930-1-9
eBook ISBN: 978-1-7356930-2-6
Library of Congress Control Number: 2020916788

Subjects: Leadership, African American Women in the Military

Think of the person you most respect and approach everyone you lead
with the same measure of respect and disposition.

Cover graphic: Studio 02
Back cover photo: Katrina Meyer Photography

For Andre,
"When I saw you I fell in love,
and you smiled because you knew."
– Arrigo Boito –

For Aliyah,
"Your crown has been bought and paid for,
all you have to do is wear it."
– James Baldwin –

For Dad,
Thank you for showing me great work ethic!

For Umm (Mom),
Thank you for sharing your love of words and music!

CONTENTS

Words from My Wingmen

"I had the privilege of working closely with CMSgt (retired) Shon Barnwell during my Air Force career and she epitomizes servant leadership in every way! This book is essential reading for anyone interested in connecting better with the people around them—so critical in these unprecedented times."

—**Brigadier General Kenneth Todorov**, USAF, Retired,
Deputy Director of the Missile Defense Agency,
Office of the Secretary of Defense, Fort Belvoir, VA.
Sector Vice President, Northrop Grumman Defense Systems

"Among the many Senior Non-Commissioned Officers I've served with, Shon set the standard for leadership and insight. Shon noted each Airman's talent and background and linked them to our mission. She jumped right in to stand up the Air Component to U.S. Africa Command. The example she showed to others was truly inspirational."

—**Brigadier General Michael W. Callan**, USAF, Retired, Vice Commander,
17th Air Force and U.S. Air Forces Africa, Ramstein Air Base, Germany

"I've served with many American heroes. Shon Barnwell is one of those leaders who rose to the top, leading at every level. Shon sees not only with her eyes but also with her heart. She is a gifted visionary thinker who adds and invests in every person she encounters. She made me a better leader!"

—**Colonel Carl F. Wood**, USAF, Deputy Chief, Hiring, Recruitment,
Staffing and Placement, National Security Agency, Fort Meade, MD

"If there were one word to describe Shon, I would say "fire", because of her amazingly positive energy, honesty, and integrity. It is rare these days to find selfless leaders who are truly energetic motivators. Shon's inspirational vision, transparency, humility, and IQ are the blueprint for developing great leaders for generations to come."

—**Chief Master Sergeant Linda Bynum**, USAF, Retired, Headquarters Air Force Reserve Command, Management Engineering Team, Robins Air Force Base, GA

"Whether we sat in comfort and safety stateside; or amid on-going rocket and mortar attacks in Central Iraq, her leadership has always set her apart. The title of this book says it all! Behavior sets the tone and example for those around us. Shon sets the tone and continues to do so!"

—**Chief Master Sergeant Daniel L. France**, USAF, Retired, Command Chief Master Sergeant, 347th Rescue Wing (Moody Air Force Base, GA) & 332d Air Expeditionary Wing (Balad Air Base, Iraq)

"Shon is a passionate advocate for holding leaders accountable for how they treat others. She is an inspiring example of leadership in action — each of us can learn from her. This book is an essential tool kit for leaders at all levels of an organization charged with caring for people."

—**Chief Master Sergeant Lorenzo Anastasie**, USAF, Retired, Command Chief Master Sergeant, 116th Air Control Wing, Robins Air Force Base, GA

"Shon's influence and confidence exceeded those in higher ranks. However, she epitomized humility and respect for her leadership. She saw potential in others, coached them to achieve greatness, and cheered all along the way! Her servant leadership inspired me to achieve several professional and personal accomplishments."

—**Dr. Terran K. Jones**, Chief Master Sergeant, USAF, Retired, Group Superintendent, 11th Mission Support Group, Joint Base Andrews, MD

"Shon's leadership is one of unsurpassed and unwavering care and compassion. She is equally committed to caring for her team and the mission. Shon's natural leadership style makes it easy for those she leads to eagerly go above and beyond their pursuits. May your leadership continue to positively impact those you lead!"

—**Chief Master Sergeant Darrel Ford**, USAF, Retired, 8th Maintenance Squadron, Kunsan Air Base, Korea

"An effective leader can direct, motivate, and inspire a team towards a particular goal. When I'm searching for the traits that an excellent leader must have, I think of Shon Barnwell. I have known her for more than 20 years and would follow her lead in any venture—she is impressive."

—**Senior Master Sergeant Wanda Janvier**, USAF, Retired, Bahrain Community School, Manama, Bahrain

"Shon truly embodied emotional intelligence before it became a buzz-word. She was the first person to give me effective and honest feedback that promoted open, two-way communication. Our Air Force continues to benefit from her positive impact on so many Capital "A" Airmen."

—**Senior Master Sergeant Latonia Booze**, USAF, former First Sergeant, United States Air Force Honor Guard, Joint Base Anacostia-Bolling, DC

"I believe a great leader not only knows when to give advice but also knows when to listen. Because Shon is so observant she knows how to uniquely apply the leadership style that suits each individual she leads. She is the type of leader that everyone needs on their team."

—**Master Sergeant Flora Ford**, USAF, Retired, Contracting Specialist, Department of Veteran Affairs, Columbia, SC

"Being away from my family for the first time was very difficult. I thought about all the things I would miss and felt overwhelmed with guilt. I wasn't the only mother on our team—there were four of us—and we all had similar concerns. After one particular call home, I felt so helpless, but I was trying to hold it together. Shon asked the team to leave the office seconds before I broke down. She offered counsel and solace. I'll never forget that day because Shon's compassionate approach and caring advice was so appreciated."

—**Technical Sergeant Rhonda Brown-Strong**, USAF, Retired, 8th Force Support Squadron, Manpower and Organization Office, Kunsan Air Base, Korea

"If there are people in the world more genuinely optimistic and caring than Shon, they are few."

—**Eddie Binder**, Founder and Principal, Apex Growth Strategies

"It's almost impossible to identify an organization in Middle Georgia that Shon has not led, managed, or mentored. Shon does it all! Removing obstacles, counseling people, and giving guidance to the community she serves are at the core of her being. I'm truly inspired by Shon's energy and follow-through. Her light is a beacon that has helped me and everyone she touches to learn, grow, and become all we can be. Thanks for the love, Shon!"

—**John Rucker**, Leadership Robins Region Class of 2015, Warner Robins, GA

"Shon is a powerhouse, but most importantly, she is authentic, passionate, and caring. She does not take her strengths as a leader for granted and she constantly works to be at her best and encourage all she touches to reach beyond their potential."

—**Meghan Florkowski**, Director, Women Igniting the Spirit of Entrepreneurship (WISE) Women's Business Center, Syracuse, NY

"Shon presents ideas to others and allows them to develop solutions that will work for the group's best interest. When I sought her assistance with my family reunion, Shon presented ideas I had not considered. She worked out all obstacles to make the event successful. She is genuinely a focused leader!"

—**Master Sergeant Celeste Rogers**, Air National Guard, Retired

"I know Shon to care passionately for others. Her commitment, enthusiasm, and energy are evident. I am excited to see how this amazing work will impact the lives of those who read it."

—**Shaw Blackmon**, Representative, Georgia District 146

"When I think of leadership, I think of integrity. Someone that you know is a loyal friend and trusted ally. I also think of compassion. Someone who is willing to invest in their people. But most importantly, I think of authenticity. Someone who keeps it real and never forgets where they came from. All of these wonderful aspects and characteristics sum up Shon Barnwell. A fellow Chief, a fellow Airman, and most importantly, a great friend!"

—**Chief Master Sergeant Manny Piñeiro**, USAF, Retired, Headquarters Air Force, First Sergeant Special Duty Manager, "Diamond 1", Pentagon, Washington, D.C.

Acknowledgements

Many hands, minds, and hearts have poured into me during my upbringing, military career, and entrepreneurial journey— and for that, I am eternally grateful. Sending a thunderous salute to the Men and Women of the …

833d Supply Squadron, Holloman Air
Force Base, New Mexico

600th Supply Squadron, Torrejon Air Base, Spain

86th Supply Squadron, Ramstein Air Base, Germany

347th Supply Squadron, Moody Air Force Base, Georgia

347th Wing, Moody Air Force Base, Georgia

347th Rescue Wing, Moody Air Force Base, Georgia

347th Mission Support Squadron,
Moody Air Force Base, Georgia

332d Air Expeditionary Wing, Balad Air Base, Iraq

8th Mission Support Squadron, Kunsan Air Base, Korea

23rd Mission Support Squadron,
Moody Air Force Base, Georgia

455th Air Expeditionary Wing, Bagram Air Field, Afghanistan

17 AF/A1, Ramstein Air Base, Germany

HQ USAFE/A1, Ramstein Air Base, Germany

HQ AFRC/A1, Robins Air Force Base, Georgia

78th Force Support Squadron,
Robins Air Force Base, Georgia

Robins Regional Chamber of Commerce, Georgia

Institute for Veterans and Military Families (IVMF)

Veteran Women Igniting the Spirit of
Entrepreneurship (V-WISE)

Entrepreneurship Bootcamp for Veterans (EBV) at UCONN

Sending love to my beautiful clients,
family members, and friends!

My Best Leadership Advice

How do leaders behave? They engineer success by practicing a concept I call AIR: action, impact, and result. Leaders take **action** to hone the individual attributes of themselves and others. Their action creates an **impact** that positively changes behavior. The **result** triggers an enriched shift in the persons' awareness, confidence, expertise, knowledge, ingenuity, talent, and skills. I successfully use the AIR leadership strategy in mentoring and coaching sessions, motivating team members, and enhancing personal relationships.

Leaders influence change through their behavior. They can build life-long relationships because they are trustworthy and respected. They keep their word and go the extra mile. In every leadership role—at work, on committees, in groups, or with your families—I offer my most impactful leadership advice:

#1 – Be a voice for the voiceless.

#2 – Be fair and consistent in all matters.

#3 – Surround yourself with good people.

#4 – Don't ask people to do something you wouldn't do.

Lead with AIR: **A**ction, **I**mpact, and **R**esults!

Foreword

Shon and I first met when she was leading the Manpower and Organization team at Kunsan Air Base, Korea; an Air Force F-16 Fighting Falcon base with a mission to take the fight North. I visited her office as a member of the Inspector General team to ensure readiness and efficiency of every aspect of her unit.

All Kunsan Air Base personnel are on a one-year unaccompanied tour, meaning they are there without family. Due to this fact, Shon wore many hats. Not only was she the team's chief, she was counselor, mentor, consoler, cheerleader, and confidant to many who were away from their families. It was evident her team and commanders trusted her implicitly. I was impressed by Shon's professionalism and visionary skills from the moment we met. She exuded the three Air Force core values of:

1) Integrity First
2) Service Before Self
3) Excellence In All We Do

Shon is an articulate communicator, thinks rationally, and has a passion to see others succeed. She does it all with a flair of inspiration and levity by using unique leadership approaches to diffuse stressful situations. One example occurred when she placed crayons and coloring books in the break room to help people relax. It worked amazingly well!

I have a genuine personal and professional respect for Shon. She leads by example and brings optimism, passion, and positive synergy to any situation. Shon's success is proven; she attained the rank of Chief Master Sergeant in the United States Air Force. This grade is earned by only one percent of the enlisted force.

I consider Shon a colleague and friend. She always presents a trustworthy, self-motivated attitude using compassion, intelligence, and empathy to solve problems. No doubt her writings outline her methodologies. I am honored to be a part of this project.

—Chief Master Sergeant M. Lou Wetzel, USAF, Retired,
United States Pacific Air Force Command,
Manpower and Personnel Functional
Hickam Air Force Base, Hawaii
(Renamed as Joint Hickam Base Pearl Harbor-Hickam)

Introduction

The truth is, I should never have …

> launched an event planning company
>
> reached the rank of Chief Master Sergeant
>
> earned a master's degree
>
> visited/lived in 26 countries
>
> experienced 29 joyful years (and counting) of marriage
>
> had a child *after* marriage
>
> graduated 3rd in my high school class
>
> left the city of Detroit
>
> or lived!

In 1966, my mother fled her parents' home at 17 years of age into the arms of a 50-year-old hustler and numbers runner on the East Side of Detroit. I was born a year later on December 24, 1967 and raised in an apartment adjacent to Dot & Etta's Shrimp Hut on Mack Avenue and Holcomb. By age six, my sister, Sharisma and I lived in a house on Anderdon Street off Mack Avenue with our dad. Our brother, Julius lived with our maternal grandparents. I wouldn't see my mother for another two years. Those days are a blur of chasing ice-cream trucks in the summer; playing hopscotch, tag, and Red Light, Green Light in the fall; making angels in the snow during the winter; and going to the nearby ballparks to watch local baseball teams in the spring.

I remember making number runs with my dad to restaurants, pool halls, and bars. I also remember spending countless Sundays at storefront churches. Regrettably, I remember the day police officers came to our house because our dad left us unattended one time too many. We were turned over to Child Protective Services and taken to a group home. I remember our dad never being the same after the separation. He smiled less, was always nervous and untrusting, and began telling us that no one would ever take us away from him again. I remember the feeling of sadness from seeing his broken spirit. At the age of eight, I also remember the shame I felt because I opened the door for the police officers.

Once we were back in our dad's custody, he worked tirelessly to care for us over the next few years. But by the age of 58, he was becoming more forgetful and prone to hallucinations. When an aunt found two small nooses in his briefcase, she intervened. We went to live with our maternal grandparents—Allen and Annie Bell Cheeks—on the East Side of Detroit. Our grandparents migrated north from Prattville, Alabama in search of better economic opportunities. They found jobs as automotive factory workers and worked for General Motors and Chrysler until retirement.

While our grandparents worked, I was the law, judge, and jury from 7:00 a.m. – 5:00 p.m. I would order my siblings and cousins into the sunroom and magically become a schoolteacher—or principal if the "class" was unruly. Our grandparents, both sharecroppers from the south, ensured we each had enough chores to keep the devil at bay. I can still hear my grandmother say, "An idle mind is the devil's workshop!" They both stressed the importance of behaving properly and getting good grades at the schoolhouse. Trust me, you never wanted anyone from Nichols or Trix Elementary or Fred M. Butzel Middle School calling with unpleasant news. Our granddad was 6'3" and probably weighed 300 pounds. As a child, his leather belt looked as if it could loop the entire Earth!

We lived with our mother on the West Side of Detroit in small Muslim communities. Our mother's stints of appearances were angrily greeted with Grandma uttering not-so-nice words. She'd call her shiftless, trifling, and lazy—words I never wanted anyone to hurl in my direction. During the third summer, our mother moved to an upper flat on the East Side of the city.

At the new location, we were not allowed to speak with any non-Muslim people. Nor could we contact any of our relatives. We entered into a new lifestyle: learning Arabic and the pillars of Islam, praying five times a day, dressing in a new way, and bonding with our new Muslim sisters. I enjoyed our new lives until my mother announced I'd soon marry a man who was 35 years old. I was 12 years of age. When the non-Muslim family members of my soon-to-be husband heard the news, they beat him miserably. They were appalled that a man of his age would consider marrying a minor.

Once the commotion faded, I convinced my mother to allow me to visit my dad at his nursing home. I was to return at 7 p.m. Unfortunately, I didn't realize the bus line stopped running after sunset. Feeling uneasy in a strange place, I called the only phone number I knew. Within 30 minutes, my Uncle Kojack and Aunt Lenora arrived and pleaded with me to tell them where we lived. As my uncle drove to the house to retrieve my sister, my aunt fired questions like a machine gun shooting ammunition. Her next question came before I could completely answer the current question.

"Why haven't you call us before now? Who are the people at the house where you are staying? How many men live there? Have any of the men touched you or your sister? Do they have guns? Is this the first time you've been able to leave the house?" After 30 minutes, we arrived at the house. Toting his .45 handgun in plain sight, my uncle retrieved my sister from the upper flat with no resistance. We silently departed into nightfall.

Aunt Lenora called a family gathering to decide where my sister and I would live. She would take me in and recommended another aunt take my sister. Our mother's youngest sister Bernadine had babysat us as toddlers and wouldn't hear of our separation. She and her husband at the time, Jefferey, became our legal guardians and my sister and I moved into their home. For the first time since being a toddler, we were in a cohesive family unit. We also had three new brothers – Jefferey Jr., Deon, and Jevale. That night I was able to sleep in a bed for the first time in four years over a makeshift pallet on the floor.

"Make your mess your message."

- Robin Roberts, American broadcaster

How to Use This Book

Three questions every exceptional leader can answer about their people are:

1. What's their next big thing?
2. What keeps them up at night?
3. What brings them joy?

How do you obtain answers to these questions? You make a sincere effort to know your people!

The leadership qualities addressed in this book apply to every area of life—work, family, friends, social clubs, and affiliations. Use the homework assignments at the end of each chapter to help you lead with AIR: **A**ction, **I**mpact, and **R**esults!

Action —'akSH(ə)n | Noun | The fact or process of doing something, typically to achieve an aim.

Impact —'im,pakt | Noun | The effect or influence of one person, thing, or action, on another.

Result —rə'zəlt | Noun | A consequence, effect, or outcome of something.

All definitions were retrieved from Lexico.com

The Chief's Creed

Chief Master Sergeants are individually to be regarded as people:

Who cannot be bought

Whose word is their bond

Who put character above wealth

Who possess opinions and a will

Who are larger than their vocations

Who will not lose their individuality in a crowd

Who do not hesitate to take chances

Who will be as honest in small things as in great ones

Who will make no compromise with wrong

Whose ambitions are not confined to their own selfish desires and interests

Who are true to their friends throughout good report and evil report, in adversity as well as prosperity

Who do not believe that shrewdness, cunning, and hard-headedness are the best qualities for winning success

Who are not ashamed or afraid to stand for the truth when it is unpopular,

Who can say "no" with emphasis, although all the world is saying "yes."

Lakota Legend of the Dreamcatcher

As a retired Chief, I wanted to include in this book symbolism that speaks to destiny and positive energy. The image featured on each chapter page is known as a Dreamcatcher.

Long ago, when the world was young, an old Lakota spiritual leader was on a high mountain and had a vision. In his vision, Iktomi—the great trickster and teacher of wisdom—appeared in the form of a spider. Iktomi spoke to him in a sacred language that only spiritual leaders of the Lakota could understand. As Iktomi spoke, he took the elder's willow hoop—which had feathers, horse hair, and beads on it—and began to spin a web.

He spoke to the elder about the cycles of life: we begin our lives as infants, then childhood, and then adulthood. Finally, we grow old and must be cared for as infants, thus, completing the cycle. "But," Iktomi said as he continued to spin his web, "in each phase of life there are many forces—some good and some bad. If you listen to the good forces, they will steer you in the right direction. But, if you listen to the bad forces, they will hurt you and steer you in the wrong direction."

He continued, "There are many forces and different directions that can help or interfere with the harmony of nature and also with the Great Spirit and all of his wonderful teachings." All while the spider spoke, he continued to weave his web starting from the outside and working toward the center. When Iktomi finished speaking, he gave the Lakota elder the web and said, "See, the web is a perfect circle, with a hole in the center of the circle."

"Use the web to help yourself and your people to reach your goals and make use of your people's ideas, dreams, and visions. If you believe in the Great Spirit, the web will catch your good ideas, and the bad ones will go through the hole." The Lakota elder passed his vision on to his people. Traditionally, a dreamcatcher is hung above beds or placed in homes to sift dreams and visions.

Chapter 1

Character and Courage

Be a lamp, a lifeboat,
or a ladder.

- Rumi
Persian Poet

I was born on December 24 in Detroit, Michigan, months after the 1967 Riots. Most of my family members worked for one of the Big Three automotive factories—Fiat Chrysler, Ford Motor, or General Motors. Our elders expected us to be good students, make passing grades, be respectful, and get a good job. Our East Side neighborhood contained working-class people—both Black and White—who praised our academic successes and watched over us as surrogate parents. They would also voice their disappointment or disapproval when we misbehaved. My most severe youthful infractions were riding my bike in the street, walking on a neighbor's lawn, or picking roses from someone's prized rosebush. That is until I went to an elementary school in the suburbs.

Around 1975, the city bussed a group of kids from our street, Anderdon, and a few surrounding streets to Trix Elementary School. The school was surrounded by lovely brick homes with well-maintained yards and trees that formed canopies over the streets. The school was a stately brown brick building, and the teachers were pleasant but firm. The only difference between our former school and Trix was the 30-minute bus ride and the mass of white students who lined the sidewalks as we exited the bus each day. As the weeks progressed, I became friends with a fellow second-grader named Tommie. He was friendly, and we both loved to race. He was smaller than the average second-grader, but what he lacked in height, he made up for in speed!

One day during recess, one of the older kids from our neighborhood challenged the two of us to a race. We gladly accepted. We quickly moved to our improvised starting line—usually a person facing the racers with their arms held out straight to resemble the letter "T." The person started the countdown, "On your mark, get set, GO!"

Off we went, pumping our arms and churning our legs as fast as we could. Midway to the finish line—where another human "T" stood—someone tripped Tommie, and the playground erupted with laughter. The sound of gravel making a small trench under Tommie's body made me change my course and run back to him. He lay face down, on the verge of sobbing. I helped him to his feet and dusted his freshly scraped hands as he steadied his body. Then we gave each other "the look." The only cardinal sin of a footrace is not to finish. Determined not to become the first racers in Trix history to wear the footrace badge of shame, we hobbled together across the finish line, making sure we each touched the hand of the human "T."

As we walked toward the gymnasium doors, in total silence, both in tears, I knew I had achieved something significant that day. I listened to my inner voice that said, "Always help someone who needs it." As we boarded the bus that afternoon, I quickly took my seat. When the person who tripped Tommie during the footrace approached, the bus jerked, and I swung my leg into the aisle. The bully tumbled forward and the entire bus erupted into laughter.

Leaders are bold, brave, and fearless! Our responsibility to others and ourselves is to display character when no one is watching and exude courage when the world is watching. I no longer use revengeful tactics to deal with difficult personalities. Instead, I first attempt to directly address the issue with the person to understand what is really driving their behavior. The goal is to develop a relationship based on professionalism and mutual respect. Through life experiences and practice, I exercise personal courage when dealing with bullies. Most importantly, I always stand up for someone unable to self-advocate regardless of the circumstances or consequences.

"Courage is the gift of character."

- Euripides, Greek dramatist

Chapter 1 Homework: Character and Courage

#Recall | When did you most recently display courage or help someone face a difficult situation?

_____

_____

_____

_____

_____

_____

_____

_____

_____

_____

_____

_____

_____

_____

_____

_____

_____

_____

_____

_____

#Relate | How did your actions benefit others, your team, or organization?

_____

_____

_____

_____

_____

_____

_____

_____

_____

_____

_____

_____

_____

_____

_____

_____

_____

_____

_____

_____

_____

#Act | How will you create a legacy of outstanding courage and character?

_____

_____

_____

_____

_____

_____

_____

_____

_____

_____

_____

_____

_____

_____

_____

_____

_____

_____

_____

_____

Chapter 2

Optimistic

Every day may not be good, but there's something good in every day.

- Author unknown

arrived at Lackland Air Force Base, Texas, in November 1988 to a mass of screaming Training Instructors (TIs). My most vivid memory from Day Number One is hearing the TIs say, "Pick 'em up; set 'em down!" If you arrived at basic training with luggage, you instantly realized the error of your decision. After several hours of hauling our baggage around the training grounds and the constant up and down motion from handling the bags, most trainees were ready to dump them in the trash! One TI marched us past a dumpster and asked if anyone wanted to "lighten their load." As the day came to a close, I remember thinking that it was better to have the items in my bag and not need them than to need them and not have them!

Yes, ladies and gentlemen, my optimistic attitude carried me through every mental and physical challenge in basic training—and continues to do so today. When we marched for hours on the drill pad, I found joy in mastering the maneuvers with precision. When I was on the dormitory laundry detail, I was grateful for a change of scenery. Experiencing the outdoors after sunset, hearing cars drive by, and feeling the crisp breeze of winter nights on my face was refreshing. When we completed the obstacle course, I was thankful for every aching muscle because I became physically and mentally stronger. When our lead TI named me and a few other trainees "Chunky Chickens," I delighted in my final weigh-in because I lost 17 pounds. And when another TI threatened to make me repeat training for "eyeballing" (a bold stare), I rejoiced in being recognized as a Basic Military Training School Honor Graduate.

Regardless of what happens in life, what matters the most is how you choose to view the journey. Leaders who view obstacles as growth opportunities generate solutions and innovative protocols. Leaders who evaluate setbacks and improve processes have the ability to benchmark practices for entire industries. Leaders who embrace their team's diversity by creating inclusive work cultures and investing in all team members tend to develop high-performing teams. When we remain optimistic, we allow ourselves to learn something from everyone and every circumstance.

"Perpetual optimism is a force multiplier."
- Colin Powell, 65th U.S. Secretary of State

Chapter 2 Homework: Optimistic

#Recall | When did you most recently showcase optimism?

_____

_____

_____

_____

_____

_____

_____

_____

_____

_____

_____

_____

_____

_____

_____

_____

_____

_____

_____

_____

_____

_____

_____

#Relate | How did you benefit from your optimistic attitude?
How did others benefit?

_____

_____

_____

_____

_____

_____

_____

_____

_____

_____

_____

_____

_____

_____

_____

_____

_____

_____

_____

_____

_____

#Act | What phrases, quotes, or affirmations do you use to keep thinking positively?

_____

_____

_____

_____

_____

_____

_____

_____

_____

_____

_____

_____

_____

_____

_____

_____

_____

_____

_____

_____

_____

List a few activities that boost your positivity.

_____

_____

_____

_____

_____

_____

_____

_____

_____

_____

_____

_____

_____

_____

_____

_____

_____

_____

_____

_____

_____

_____

_____

Chapter 3

Leadership

Be truthful, gentle,
and fearless.

- Mahatma Gandhi
Activist

Take a moment to recall the first person that demonstrated impactful and positive leadership in your life or career. Once you have that vision, what experience do you vividly remember? How did the person you make you feel? How well did they know your strengths and vulnerabilities? Over time, did they guide and motivate you as you gained new knowledge and skills? Did they take action, engineer an impact for success, and produce a favorable result? Indeed they made every effort to prepare you for success. As your confidence increased, did the person pushed you beyond your comfort zone? An effective leader ensures people are well trained, positioned for excellence, and encouraged to take leaps of faith. They hone awareness, confidence, expertise, knowledge, ingenuity, talent, and skills. The first Senior Non-Commissioned Officer to significantly impact my Air Force career was Master Sergeant Kim E. Keith.

After basic training, I was assigned to the 833d Supply Squadron (#SupSup). In January 1989, I headed off to Holloman Air Force Base in Alamogordo, New Mexico. In my new career, I would learn the duties of a warehouseman—or box kicker, our common nickname. My responsibilities included storing all supplies and equipment, providing secure storage for classified and sensitive items, selecting property for issue or shipment, performing daily warehouse functions, and maintaining good housekeeping and safety practices. We stored more than 26,000 line items valued at 20 million dollars to support 72 F-15 aircraft and 125 AT-38 aircraft. I took my box-kicking role to maintain our 50,000-square-foot warehouse seriously.

I enjoyed the solitary hours spent in bin rows stacked 40 feet high in some locations and over 100 feet in length. Time spent selecting thousands of items—washers, bolts, nuts, screws, seals, fasteners, tires, and other components—gives you a lot of time to think and plan your future. I particularly loved—yes, loved—keeping the bin labels properly affixed and updated. I was joyful when rows were clean, and boxes were kept flush with the edge of shelves, and inventory accuracy was 100%. Within a few short months, Sergeant Keith had me demonstrate to the team techniques for maintaining the bin rows. After I received a glowing inspection rating, he had me inspect the work of others. By the summer, I was called upon to present impromptu training sessions during our weekly staff meetings. When Base Supply briefed Distinguished Visitors (DVs), I was nominated to showcase the Storage and Issue Section.

Now, to be clear, I wasn't all too happy to be the main person taking on these additional roles. I often felt that Sergeant Keith was picking on me, and I frequently vented my perceived unfair treatment to my peers. "Why did I have so many tasks on my plate? Why couldn't I do my job and leave at 1630 (4:30 p.m.) like everyone else?" The pressure to be responsive, reliable, engaged, and professional—all the time—was, at times, very overwhelming. At these moments, I'd hear my dear grandmother's voice saying, "That chile is a hard and strong worker. She can do anything she sets her mind to do!" Her voice would make me perk up and keep going. Then, one day, a team member backed out of a quarterly awards event, and I had a one-day notice to prep to meet the awards panel.

During an awards panel, a group of three to five people presented questions from a 15-chapter book called the Promotion Fitness Examination (PFE). The PFE covered Air Force history, customs and courtesies, leadership, professionalism, and various topics. Plus, there was always a current events question. We earned points for dress and appearance, so your uniform had to be sharp. Your military bearing had to be impeccable. People would spend months preparing to "meet the board."

I was devastated to have only one day of preparation to meet the board. It felt as if I was being thrown to the wolves. When I told Sergeant Keith I wouldn't meet the board; he pushed back and told me I had no choice. I voiced my disappointment and was near tears. Before losing all decorum, Senior Master Sergeant Bracey—the highest ranking enlisted member of our section—entered the hallway. I must note, a Senior Master Sergeant (E-8), also referred to as "Senior," was a near-god-like entity to an Airman First Class (E-3). Senior Bracey asked a straightforward question, "Airman Carpenter, what is your greatest fear?" I was stunned for two reasons: 1) He knew my name and 2) This was the first time he'd spoken directly to me. My thoughts tumbled for several minutes before I replied, "I don't want to let the team down." Senior Bracey responded, "We selected you to represent the section, so you are already a winner!" As swiftly as he appeared, he returned to his office.

Over the next few months, I won the Deputy Commander for Resource Management and the 833d Supply Airman of the Quarter award, and competed for the Twelfth Air Force Supply Airman of the Quarter. Throughout my assignment at Holloman Air Force Base, I received many accolades and awards: the Holloman Air Force Base Chiefs' Look Sharp Award, Supply Squadron Best Training Class of the Month, Storage and Issue Person of the Month, and Woman of the Year at Holloman Air Force Base nominee. When Colonel Hart, the Chief of Supply, reviewed the records of all Senior Airman Below-the-Zone candidates—a program where you are promoted to E-4 six months early—he had the option of promoting four people. He only selected one—Airman First Class Shon Carpenter! At that moment, I realized why my leadership continuously motivated and encouraged me to always go the extra mile. They understood the power of preparing people for their next big thing, even when the individual is not able to envision their greatness.

My experiences under the leadership of Sergeant Keith and Senior Bracey continue to drive my love for talent management. They groomed their replacements in the world of Supply—a career field that I would serve in for over 10 years. They highlighted the importance of mentoring those who don't look like you—our team of 12 people had three women assigned. Sergeant Keith created unimaginable goals and expected everyone to excel. He was smart, challenging, and fair, and I knew I wanted to be that type of leader one day.

"Run to the fire; don't hide from it."
- Meg Whitman
Chief Executive Officer (CEO) of Quibi
Former CEO of Hewlett Packard and eBay

Chapter 3 Homework: Leadership

#Recall | What traits do you display as a leader?

_____

_____

_____

_____

_____

_____

_____

_____

_____

_____

_____

_____

_____

_____

_____

_____

_____

_____

_____

_____

_____

_____

#Relate | How do others benefit from your time, talent, and tenacity as a leader? Have you ever seen something in someone that they didn't see in themselves?

_____

_____

_____

_____

_____

_____

_____

_____

_____

_____

_____

_____

_____

_____

_____

_____

_____

_____

_____

_____

_____

#Act | What trait(s) would you like to hone to enhance your ability to help others succeed?

_____

_____

_____

_____

_____

_____

_____

_____

_____

_____

_____

_____

_____

_____

_____

_____

_____

_____

_____

_____

Think of someone you are currently leading, coaching, or mentoring. Outline how you are using **AIR** to provide leadership:

A—Action | What action will you take?

_____

_____

_____

_____

I—Impact | What impact will your action(s) have?

_____

_____

_____

_____

R—Result | What is the final result?

_____

_____

_____

_____

_____

_____

_____

_____

_____

_____

_____

_____

Chapter 4

Emotional Intelligence

We see things not as they are, but as we are. Our perception is shaped by our precious experiences.

- Dr. Dennis Kimbro
Author and Professor

I arrived at Torrejon Air Base in Spain in 1991, newly married and excited to experience a new culture. I loved the frantic traffic circles and the vastness of the Prado Museum in Madrid. I delighted in the variety of El Rastro flea markets—fantastic food, art, music, books, clothing, amazing leather goods, and lively people. I stood in awe of the timeless architecture. I loved our chalet in the village of Daganzo and often drove to local villages to photograph murals. I loved the multitude of festivals, the richness of the culture, and the practicality of siestas. I loved everything about being in Spain with one exception—I didn't like the Sergeant assigned to the Pick-Up and Delivery Section because she was a bully!

In the beginning, she made snide comments about little things—my handwriting, my uniform, my "big city" accent. Whenever I was offloading a vendor's truck, she'd ask if I was qualified to drive a 10,000-pound load capacity forklift. After a few months, her comments progressed to character assassination and sabotage. Sergeant Bully attempted to create doubt in my abilities by telling higher ranking people I didn't know my job very well. She would also demand I quote the name and content of regulations related to property transfer or handling procedures. When I currently stated the regulation, she'd reply, "Oh, I was just joking, you didn't have to answer that question." Almost weekly, a member of her section would strike up a conversation with me. "You haven't heard it from me, but I overheard her talking smack about you to a group of people in the front office." When I'd mention the comments to my supervisor, he'd ask me to overlook her behavior because "she's very well-liked." Then he'd add,

"You don't want any problems with her." I was so agitated I could chew steel.

The major showdown occurred over the transfer of classified property. When handling classified property, there must be a continuous custody of receipt. Every person receiving the item must be listed on a classified property roster and provide proof of identity—no exceptions. Upon receipt of the priority—Mission Capable (MICAP)—document, I called the Pick-Up and Delivery Section to have an authorized team member meet me. Then, I retrieved the appropriate roster and headed to the vault. When I arrived at the vault, there was Sergeant Bully. When I asked for her ID card, she refused to show it and stated, "Just pull the property, you know who I am!" When I refused to open the vault, she shouted, "Give me the damn property before we bust our delivery time!" Again I refused to open the vault and told Sergeant Bully that I was returning to my office to elevate the matter through the chain of command.

As we stepped away from the vault, Senior Master Sergeant Marcus McCain appeared—I guess he heard all the shouting. Sergeant Bully told him I was being difficult, didn't know my job, and refused to follow orders. Then he asked to hear my position. She was enraged and began pacing. Senior McCain told her to "lead by example—starting now—by following proper protocol." She angrily produced her ID card, and I retrieved the item from the vault. As I departed, I overheard Senior McCain tell Sergeant Bully to report to his office in 10 minutes with her supervisor. Of course, I don't know whether or not Sergeant Bully faced any measure of reprimand for her behavior after the incident. Since no one reported any more "overheard conversations," I was relieved.

Sergeant Bully displayed behaviors of an emerging leader in need of training and guidance. Senior Master Sergeant McCain perfectly demonstrated the impact of leaders exhibiting Emotional Intelligence, or EI. The concept speaks to a person's capacity to be aware of, control, and express one's emotions and handle interpersonal relationships reasonably and empathetically. Because of his willingness to listen to both sides of the situation, I embrace Stephen Covey's Habit #5 of highly effective people: Seek first to understand, then to be understood. When leaders listen, acknowledge, and affirm others' viewpoints, they build a foundation of trust and understanding.

**"In a very real sense we have two minds,
one that thinks and one that feels."**

- Dr. Daniel Goleman
Author and Psychologist

Chapter 4 Homework: Emotional Intelligence

#Recall | As a leader, when was the last time you made a conscious effort to view issues from the perspective of a subordinate?

_____

_____

_____

_____

_____

_____

_____

_____

_____

_____

_____

_____

_____

_____

_____

_____

_____

_____

_____

In a relationship, when was the last time you viewed an issue from the perspective a loved one?

_____

_____

_____

_____

_____

_____

_____

_____

_____

_____

_____

_____

_____

_____

_____

_____

_____

_____

_____

_____

_____

_____

Was your response positive? If your response was negative, what will you do differently the next time?

_____

_____

_____

_____

_____

_____

_____

_____

_____

_____

_____

_____

_____

_____

_____

_____

_____

_____

_____

_____

_____

_____

#Relate | Did your perspective change? Explain why.

_____

_____

_____

_____

_____

_____

_____

_____

_____

_____

_____

_____

_____

_____

_____

_____

_____

_____

_____

_____

_____

_____

_____

_____

#Act | In conflict management, people either avoid, alter, adapt, or accept an issue or problem. How will you continually leverage Dr. Wayne Dyer's principle and stay open to everything and attached to nothing?

Chapter 5

Visionary

You can only have two things: reasons or results.

- Les Brown
Speaker and Author

During my first tour of duty at Ramstein Air Base in Germany in 1992, I was selected to be a lead Quality Air Force Instructor. The selection process was very competitive, so I was honored to serve on the instructor cadre. A few days after the announcement, however, doubt started dominating my thoughts. I was excited to be an instructor, sharing information and insight, and shaping behavior. I was equally nervous because class attendees included many senior-ranking people.

The doubts flowed like a massive flood. Why would a Chief Master Sergeant or Colonel with decades of operational experience listen to a Staff Sergeant lecture on customer service or innovation topics? What could I possibly teach this group about taking care of their team? How would I hold their interest during our one-day training session? Would this yearlong quest end as a major failure or a brilliant success?

I accessed my creativity—gained early in my career when Master Sergeant Keith picked me to conduct impromptu training sessions. Then, I thoughtfully evaluated my facilitation skills—developed as a youngster looking over my siblings after school while our grandparents worked. Certainly, I possessed the skills to be successful as an instructor regardless of the training attendees' rank or knowledge. I reflected on the hours spent preparing for award panels and promotion exams—my discipline and dedication were indeed intact. Although the senior leaders had years of learned experiences, I brought new and diverse perspectives on processes, technology, and business practices to the discussion. The moment I decided not to allow fear to paralyze me from moving forward, I stepped out of my comfort zone, and magic happened! I leveraged my talent and tenacity to lead boldly.

At the time, I was an avid tennis player, so I decided to use tactics from the sport to relay quality concepts. Even if most of the attendees never played tennis before, they'd witnessed highlights of professional players on a sports outlet or two. When we discussed strategy, I would ask the group which tennis players had the best serve. I'd then ask the group what elements of the serve were effective. Some responses included speed, shock value, ball placement, and surprise. Instantly, the group began sharing stories on how delayed responses to priorities adversely impacted their organizations (bad news never gets better with time). Others identified how advanced planning and training allowed the unit to stretch limited resources or anticipate surges or challenges.

Next, I'd introduce the concept of "court presence" by drawing a tennis court on the board. I'd solicit comments from the group based on a variety of scenarios. I'd ask the group what action they would take if they stood close to the net and the opposing player lobbed the ball over their head? Or what would they do if they were standing at the baseline and the returning play narrowly cleared the net? What if the player returned the ball to the opponent's left backhand, and they were too far to the right? As the discussion unfolded, the group began making analogies relating to "Where are we as a unit?" "Where do we stand in comparison to like organizations?" Also, they discussed, "Where do we need to go?" "Are we watching our blind spots?" "Are we listening to our customers—internal and external?" The conversations were very lively!

The third tennis concept presented to the group focused on "touch" to address the issue of power. When I was close to the net and the opposing player was at the baseline, I would gently tap the ball over the net for a soft return. Similarly, when leaders implement change, a soft and consistent touch is required to secure consensus, buy-in, and trust. When I caught the opposing player off-center or scurrying to regain their court presence, I'd return the volley very forcefully. When leaders must make time-sensitive decisions, they are direct, precise, and prompt.

Lastly, the final topic discussed was "mindset." I have lost many tennis matches because I failed to keep thinking positively. Beating myself up about an error on a previous play made me lose my focus, causing more mistakes. I asked the group to share how they performed in the presence of a leader with nervous energy. How effective were they when a leader constantly shifted priorities, goals, or expectations? How often were they successful when leadership didn't trust them by supporting their decisions, or more damaging, criticized them in the presence of peers or subordinates? Through our discussion of mindset, leaders were able to identify and reflect on the impact of their individual leadership styles and the use of power.

By the end of the year, I doubled my teaching requirement and helped shape the strategic Quality Training Plan for more than 1,000 people—and remained the only junior Non-Commissioned Officer on the team. Oh yeah, I also won the 1995 Ramstein Intramural Women's League Tennis Singles Title! When confronted with an unimaginable task or challenge, it helps to step back and evaluate the effort in the simplest terms possible. Review your AIR strategy: action, impact, and result. Ensure you are improving awareness, confidence, expertise, knowledge, ingenuity, talent, and skills. Thankfully, I didn't let fear dominate my decision to move out of my comfort zone to embrace a new and rewarding opportunity.

"I always did something I was a little not ready to do. I think that's how you grow. When there's that moment of 'Wow, I'm not really sure I can do this,' and you push through those moments, that's when you have a breakthrough."

- Marissa Mayer
Businesswoman and Former Chief Executive
Officer of Yahoo

Chapter 5 Homework: Visionary

#Recall | When was the last time you did something out of your comfort zone? How did you initially react? How did the experience unfold?

_____

_____

_____

_____

_____

_____

_____

_____

_____

_____

_____

_____

_____

_____

_____

_____

_____

_____

_____

_____

_____

_____

#Relate | When was the last time you encouraged someone to do something out of their comfort zone? How did they react? How did you support them through the process? What was the outcome of the experience?

_____

_____

_____

_____

_____

_____

_____

_____

_____

_____

_____

_____

_____

_____

_____

_____

_____

_____

_____

_____

_____

#Act | What would you do if you knew you could not fail?

_____

_____

_____

_____

_____

_____

_____

_____

_____

_____

_____

_____

_____

_____

_____

_____

_____

_____

_____

_____

_____

_____

_____

_____

_____

_____

Chapter 6

Inspirational

When you learn, teach.

- Maya Angelo
Author and Activist

I experienced my first combat landing in early March 2004 to Balad Air Base and Logistics Support Area (LSA) Anaconda, Iraq. We flew into the base in the early hours of darkness with chaff and flare from the aircraft brilliantly lighting the sky. It was the first time I deployed with my weapon on my person. I instantly wished I'd practice reloading my 9 MM clip in total darkness. When the aircraft landed and came to a full stop, the pilot greeted the group with "Welcome to Mortaritaville." Someone tagged the name due to the frequency of mortar attacks from nearby neighborhoods. A few of the passengers chuckled. I immediately started praying!

I deployed to Balad as a member of the 332d Air Expeditionary Wing (AEW) to stand up the first wing level Manpower Office in support of Operation IRAQI FREEDOM. Our office ensured aircraft (iron) and personnel (forces) showed up in the right number, at the right place, and at the right time. The 332d AEW spearheaded the first-ever F-16 deployment based in Iraq—10 aircraft flew 606 missions and over 21,000 hours, providing close air support for ground troops under hostile fire. Medical personnel provided essential treatment to more than 20,000 patients in Iraq, saving countless lives of U.S. service members, Iraqi civilians, and coalition allies. Over 300 tactical convoy missions covering over 250,000 miles transpired. A combat first, the wing integrated the Predator into the airbase defense plan, enabling the destruction of enemy mortar positions and causing a 90% reduction in base attacks. From May 2003 to April 2004, the 332d AEW controlled over 38,000 combat events covering the entire Iraq theater of operations. Their efforts led to successful combat missions eradicating terrorist interests in Iraq, ultimately leading to the capture of Saddam Hussein.

On April 10, 2004, nearly a month into my deployment, tent city residents were awakened shortly after midnight by the sound of rocks showering our tent and wailing sirens. Then the giant voice blared, "This is the command post. Code Red is in effect. Stay down. I say again, Code Red. Stay down." A Code Red alarm indicates an attack or hostile act is imminent or in progress. I took cover under the bed. Typically when there's one mortar attack, it's followed by one or two more blasts, causing more injuries as forces respond to the initial attack. You could hear a host of emergency response vehicles swarming by our sleeping quarters at speeds well above the mandated 5-mph in tent city. Immediately, I knew something was wrong.

Shortly after the "all clear" message on the giant voice, my supervisor appeared outside the sleeping area with his flashlight. After every attack, an accountability drill ensures all team members are safe. As I stepped out of our tent, the sight was surreal. In total darkness, all tent city residents were checking on their battle buddies. The Medics had transported injured personnel to the Contingency Aeromedical Staging Facility (CASF). The Chaplain team comforted a host of troops. Random people offered hugs and asked each other if they were okay. The civil engineers cleared debris from the mortar attack. By sunrise, a memorial marked the space where one Airman died—A1C Antoine Jermaine Holt—and two others were wounded.

The actions of countless people whose names I'll never know genuinely inspired me. I don't think anyone deployed to the 332d AEW and LSA Anaconda will ever be the same after that attack. I salute all Medics who witnessed unimaginable injuries. I salute all the Defenders and Infantry troops who protected the base—inside and outside the concertina wire. I salute the people who flew various types of aircraft: fixed, rotary, and unmanned drones. I salute every maintainer who repaired the aircraft. I salute every person who fed us and ensured housing was available. I salute the communications teams whose efforts allowed us to call family and friends back home. I salute the joint forces that processed, staged, and transported supplies, equipment, people, and mail.

I am grateful to Lieutenant Colonel James Mitnik. He supported the Manpower Office's recommendations that led to the successful bed-down of new wing missions for expeditionary combat support. I am thankful for the larger-than-life presence of Command Chief Master Sergeant Daniel France, who embraced each team member regardless of rank, gender, race, or age. I am sure he only slept three hours a night because he spent countless hours visiting and listening to troops. He made us laugh—and think outside the box—and immensely boosted morale.

It was an honor to be a part of something larger than myself! Inspirational leaders understand the importance of supporting their teams, listening to and motivating them, and showing their people a total 360-degree perspective of their actions, impacts, and results. I will always remember Colonel Marke Gibson, the 332d AEW Commander, for his leadership. He invited the entire Manpower Office to join him on the roof of our building—cigars in hand and the sunset on the horizon—to witness the first landing of A-10 Thunderbolt aircraft. A wave of pride covered me. The new aircraft would help protect friendly forces and provide supporting firepower. Our office played a pivotal role in the planning and execution process for the beddown of the A-10 aircraft.

"If your actions inspire others to dream more, learn more, do more, you are a leader."

– Simon Sinek
Author and Speaker

Chapter 6 Homework: Inspirational

#Recall | What's your most recent example of inspirational leadership? What significance does this experience play in your life?

_____

_____

_____

_____

_____

_____

_____

_____

_____

_____

_____

_____

_____

_____

_____

_____

_____

_____

_____

_____

#Relate | How will you leverage your skills and influence to lead others? How often do you inspire someone who does not look like you? Consider gender, race, ethnicity, age, education, socioeconomic group, etc.

_____

_____

_____

_____

_____

_____

_____

_____

_____

_____

_____

_____

_____

_____

_____

_____

_____

_____

_____

_____

_____

_____

#Act | What effort or project will you commit to and change for the better within the next quarter? The next year?

_____

_____

_____

_____

_____

_____

_____

_____

_____

_____

_____

_____

_____

_____

_____

_____

_____

_____

_____

_____

_____

_____

_____

Chapter 7

Effective Communicator

The soul becomes dyed with the color of its thoughts.

- Marcus Aurelius
Roman Emperor
& Philosopher

My 25-year military career demonstrated that leaders who are effective communicators pay close attention to four factors: flow of language, context, intent, and tone. Public speaking courses and clubs teach us to "know our audience" to ensure our message is clear and well-received. Seemingly innocent references can greatly impact our ability to connect with others. When executed correctly, our team members, peers, family, friends, and stakeholders have all the necessary information to take action. When we fall short, our endeavors create confusion and frustration; or worse, they make others feel belittled or offended. Throughout my career, I found that communication flowed more genuinely when I learned people's stories. Remember, Stephen Covey's 5th Habit of highly effective leaders reminds us to, "Seek first to understand, then to be understood."

When our daughter, Aliyah, was a toddler, she used words that only people who spent time with her would understand. A few words that come to mind are tank two, pam poo, and me me—her words for thank you, shampoo, and mine. When I ask family members visiting from Detroit the type of beverage they'd like me to have on hand, I use the term pop. If I'm speaking with my in-laws in South Carolina, I use the word soda. When in Georgia, I pronounce pecans as PEA-cans. When I'm in Michigan, I'll say, PAH-cons. Speaking the language that people understand allows us to connect with one another. It shapes our commitment to those we know, love, and serve. Our actions make us relatable.

As young Airmen, my crew and I used the term diss when someone disrespected another person. Today, the term used is shade. The terms fly or fresh—used to refer to a stylish or fashionable person—have been replaced with swag and drip. When we described a remarkable event or experience, we'd say something was dope. Now the term lit is prevalent. The word thirsty refers to an overly ambitious or attention-starved individual. Again, how we use language to relate to one another is imperative. As you lead people junior to you in age, status, position, or rank, ensure you speak—or are aware of—their language. The more time we spend with people, the more effectively we can communicate with them.

I have encountered leaders who did not spend time discussing operational concepts with new Airmen or entry-level personnel. The leader believed the information would fall on deaf ears. Nothing could be farther from the truth! It's not that junior members or emerging leaders don't possess the aptitude to understand the concepts. Instead, they may lack the experience or context to relate to the message. Be sure to link your organizations' strategic goals to the action, impact, and result of each team member to reinforce context.

As a newly assigned Supply troop at Holloman Air Force Base in New Mexico, I knew Mission Capable or MICAP requests were a "drop everything and move" priority. I knew there was a specific timeframe to retrieve, prepare, and deliver the item to another work center. However, I didn't understand the "why" that drove the urgency. I also didn't have a full vision of why the item was essential for the end user. After the reprimand of a team member for "busting a MICAP," a series of training sessions corrected late deliveries. Once the group understood the scenario that drove a MICAP requisition, all items arrived on time. I use that lesson to this day in training sessions to explain each warfighter's role at each level in the

Department of Defense organizational structure. This event also sparked my love for creating continuity books. These guides ensure team members understand how they fit operationally, as well as how they help the group achieve goals and objectives.

Leaders communicate with their teams to inform, reassure, seek information, motivate, and direct. The willingness to share information influences intent. When you communicate with your people, what do you hope to gain? Successfully executed projects and missions or disjointed and haphazard actions? Effective communicators realize people need all available details to make informed decisions. When teams receive the "5 Ws"—what, when, where, why, and who—successful decision making increases. Willingly sharing information enhances trust and communicates respect from senior to junior members. Being open to questions and feedback relays to team members that their inputs are valued and appreciated. Conversely, withholding information due to inflated egos, power or control issues, or fear may create disastrous results regarding group dynamics. The most dismal day I've had as a leader was when I felt my team and I played "catch up." Providing needed details and information allows people to be proactive versus reactive. Charging hell with a water pistol with no apparent relief in sight is immensely frustrating. Real leaders are mindful of their intent and share information early and often!

We've all heard the saying, "It's not what you say, but how you say it." Leaders must be aware of their tone of voice at all times. Most people know that it's usually not a good thing when a parent calls you by pronouncing your full name.

The conversation will likely be directive or punitive. Every question is rhetorical, and the goal is to make their point to correct a perceived or real problem.

When communicating, we need to take notice of the tone we use. We are lively and responsive when addressing those senior to us in rank, position, or status. We may relax our etiquette when we speak with peers. By the time we address our subordinates, how are we doing on tone? If our style is abrasive, dismissive, or uncaring, how effective is the communication? What is the impact on the person's spirit and sense of self-worth? When our tone is straightforward, professional, and sincere, the person receiving our message feels safe, engaged, worthy, and respected. At the heart of effective communication is the transferal of respect. Our words have significant impacts on all relationships, whether on the job or with those we love. When disconnects exist in the language, context, intent, or tone, we are not effectively communicating.

"Ninety percent of leadership is the ability to communicate something people want."

- Dianne Feinstein, Politician

Chapter 7 Homework: Effective Communicator

#Recall | Describe a scenario where you were affected by poor communication. Describe a recent instance where you displayed effective communication.

_____

_____

_____

_____

_____

_____

_____

_____

_____

_____

_____

_____

_____

_____

_____

_____

_____

_____

_____

_____

#Relate | How do you cope during instances of poor or ineffective communication?

_____

_____

_____

_____

_____

_____

_____

_____

_____

_____

_____

_____

_____

_____

_____

_____

_____

_____

_____

_____

_____

_____

_____

_____

#Act | For the next week, ask yourself the following questions before you communicate:

- Is it true?

- Do I have all the details?

- Is the message time-sensitive?

- What's the best way to relay the message?

- Is the message controversial or emotional?

- Have I checked my biases and conflicting agenda?

_____

_____

_____

_____

_____

_____

_____

_____

_____

_____

_____

_____

_____

_____

_____

_____

_____

Chapter 8

Integrity

You've got enemies?
Good, that means you
stood up for something
in your life.

- Eminem
Rapper and Songwriter

Aside from a team member's death or the loss of a spouse or child, fewer life events are more devastating to a military unit than a toxic workplace. If I keep this discussion authentic—some leaders aren't worth a damn! In my experience, those creating an unhealthy work culture have egos the size of planets. They are not very good listeners, they are immensely manipulative and needy, and they are arrogant. If they are not the center of attention, then there is hell to pay—especially for the person "dimming their light." They belittle the team. They alienate their group from others. They use intimidation to force people to agree to protocols that are against the person's better judgment. They are divisive, mean-spirited, and cunning, and put their interests above all things. They can display charisma and decency long enough to get what they want from someone who's not under their span of control. In most cases, they are intelligent people, but their abuse of power overshadows that attribute. They thrive on controlling every situation, even when their input or decision creates chaos. Their team is a safety net that saves them from a terrible demise in most instances. That is, until one day the pressure becomes unbearable, and a member or members of the team crash and burn.

I know all too well the stress associated with a toxic work environment. It's the most powerless feeling I've had in my adult life. Looking into the eyes of a leader who's terrorizing a group of people and not seeing a glimmer of empathy is beyond disheartening. The person makes you feel like you aren't a team player or lack the aptitude to make stellar contributions. Then there's a constant barrage of snide comments such as "Maybe you need to work harder" or "How did you get selected for this position?" You forfeit your weekends, family events and traditions, holidays, and anniversaries—everything—to ensure this person delivers success to their superiors. Each time you are near the person, it's as if your soul shatters.

When I'm in a stressful environment, music becomes my medicine. House music plays to lift my spirits. Jazz helps when I need to wind down. Old school R&B hits the playlist when I want to dance. Blues rotates when I need to create a strategy, and classical music spins when I need to meditate. Old-school rap and hip-hop always spark innovative ideas, and gospel music plays when I'm on the verge of snatching a knot in someone's ass!

During my time spent in a toxic work environment, I stopped listening to music altogether. My entire demeanor began to shift as my duty days become longer and longer. I was easily irritated and defensive. I spoke less and became very detached from others. As I drove to the base each day, my heartbeat would increase the closer I got to the main gate. At about a quarter mile away, tears would flow nonstop. When the base entrance was visible, I'd shake uncontrollably. I'd have to pull into a sparsely populated parking lot to get myself together. Self-talk became my BFF: "Come on, Shon, get it together, girl!" "Dry up these tears!" "Just two more days until Friday." "Colonel Toxic is on leave for two weeks, you can do this! Everyone is safe." I damn near became a zombie trying to make it through the day.

In addition to feeling like you're being buried alive, there is the annoying reality that everyone around you is aware of the terror! People would offer frequent condolences for the situation. Others would say, "I don't know how you work for Colonel Toxic; I couldn't tolerate that BS." The words were nearly paralyzing because I didn't have the option to quit my military career. Undoubtedly, the most saddening comments were from the peers or superiors of the toxic leader. "We know Colonel Toxic can be demanding and a bit of a challenge, but we need you to stay strong so that we can keep the morale of the office high." What? You know this person is an unsuitable leader, yet you refuse to take action? My head tumbled in dismay on several occasions. How am I ever going to survive this experience?

I chose to fight the good fight! One of the Air Force's core values is Integrity First. By embracing this value, every member of the force must do the right thing, at all times. When Colonel Toxic would order or imply I do something that didn't lend itself to integrity first, I would not comply. When ordered to take any action to undermine another person's authority, I would send an email "clarifying" the request (document). When directed to withhold information from another senior leader so the person would appear unprepared for a staff meeting, I'd send the information to the person anyway (build trust). When a team member would break down in tears or vent out of frustration, I would listen, offer advice, and vow to stand together (stay unified). I would also seek the counsel of our First Sergeant (report). When Colonel Toxic attempted to upstage any leader, the plan flopped miserably because we banded together (create allies). When it was implied— out of nowhere—that the team would be working extended hours, I'd have pizza or sandwiches delivered to the office *(stay levelheaded)*. Needless to say, Colonel Toxic was livid.

The final blow to Colonel Toxic's ego came when a team member experienced the loss of a family member. As the colonel ranted and raved about the person being away from work, I mentioned that the person was very close to their mother, so the terminal illness was incredibly distressing. Colonel Toxic looked shocked and stated, "I didn't know." Without thinking, I replied, "How could someone who's worked for you for over a year have a dying mother, and you not know that?" If the look sent my way were a bullet, it would have been a kill shot.

Two weeks later, I was provided a "professional development opportunity" and transferred to another agency. The move was bittersweet. Guilty feelings often drowned out my joy of being in a pleasant and supportive working environment. I had left my comrades behind in an unhealthy place. I spent months strategizing and networking in hopes of securing better work environments for my colleagues. I experienced bouts of anger from being "booted out" of a fulfilling role. In the end, I was thankful to have my life back. My vehicle became an all-out concert hall as I drove to and from work. The first song in the queue was John Lee Hooker's Chill Out – Things Gonna Change featuring Carlos Santana!

Integrity is one of the top qualities of an effective leader. Leaders exercise, uphold, and safeguard the soul of the team. They ensure everyone is respected while being respectful. Leaders with integrity understand the importance of trust, kindness, and, above all, selflessness. They take responsibility for their actions and are dependable. Studies show the average person will spend one-third of their lives at work—that's 90,000 hours! As leaders, we owe it to those we influence, guide, and impact to lead with confidence, humility, and a great moral compass. The Workplace Bullying Institute states 19% of American adults reported they had experienced bullying behavior at work. Another 19% said they witnessed the bullying of others. In an article on bullying, author Bruce Roselle states, "Toxic leaders are frightened leaders who have developed ineffective behaviors to cover their irrational fears." Prevention is crucial, and the process begins with hiring.

Hiring authorities and senior leaders must recognize the damage created by a toxic leader. Their hurtful behavior may compromise the health of employees by increasing depression and anxiety. Another negative impact of toxic leaders is low productivity and morale. Additionally, turnover and absenteeism can soar. An organization can also risk costly and embarrassing legal action. If you encounter a toxic leader, Roselle suggests, "Taking a breath and responding to them as calmly and rationally as you can." He recommends following up conversations with an email to summarize your understanding of decisions made or topics discussed. If the toxic behavior continues, be sure to document the nature of the abusive action, including in your notes, the date, time, location, and witnesses' names. Never isolate yourself by keeping your emotions or the abuse hidden. When needed, contact a helping agency for counseling support and other resources.

Before you reach a breaking point, transfer to a new work center, or seek new employment.

"There are many things you can lack and still steer clear of danger. Integrity isn't one of them. ... Make it clear that you will not tolerate any deviation from any of them. Then live by them."

- Michael Ray Hopkin
Lead On Purpose Blogger

Chapter 8 Homework: Integrity

#Recall | How do you display integrity in your leadership style? How do your actions benefit others, your team, or the organization?

_____

_____

_____

_____

_____

_____

_____

_____

_____

_____

_____

_____

_____

_____

_____

_____

_____

_____

#Relate | Have you been exposed to—or do you know some-one currently exposed to—a toxic work environment?

- List ways to document the treatment.

_____

_____

_____

- How can you build trust with others who know about the abuse?

_____

_____

_____

- List ways to stay unified with your team or the impacted member(s).

_____

_____

_____

- What agencies exist to report the abuse? List con-tact names, phone numbers, and emails.

_____

_____

_____

- How can you create allies to support yourself, the team, or the impacted member(s)?

_____

_____

_____

- How will you stay levelheaded? How will you encourage others to remain levelheaded?

_____

_____

_____

- List the names of two people who will "charge hell with a water pistol" with you.

_____

_____

_____

- When you need to talk, vent, or cry, call the people listed below.

_____

_____

_____

#Act | What action(s) will you take when you encounter a leader who lacks integrity?

_____

_____

_____

_____

_____

_____

_____

_____

Chapter 9

Dependable

A leader is one who knows the way, goes the way, and shows the way.

- John C. Maxwell
Author and Speaker

One of the quickest ways a leader will lose trust is by not keeping their word. When we promise to do something, we must follow through on our commitment. Merriam-Webster defines dependable as, "capable of being trusted or depended on; reliable." Ask yourself, "Who's depending on me?" If you are a member of the Armed Forces, your nation and her allies depend on you to support and defend their freedom.

The employees, shareholders, and board of directors rely on the chief executive officer to lead effectively and generate profits. Communities depend on the president of non-profit organizations to provide sound leadership as they solve problems. Taxpayers depend on the leaders of government agencies to provide resources and impactful advocacy.

Family members and friends depend on each of us for love, support, and encouragement. I believe a dependable leader takes care of themselves, their family, their team, and their boss. They also manage conflict and lead by example. Lastly, they transition gracefully from their leadership role to another position or retirement.

One day, I left my home at 5:30 a.m., headed to the office, and didn't leave until 1:00 a.m. the next day. I knew I had a problem. My long duty hours didn't begin all at once. I've assessed that I logged 14-to-16-hour days, six days a week, during the last eight years of my military career. Don't get me wrong; I wasn't at work for that length of time for fear of missing out. Nor was I the type of leader who lost unused vacation days at the end of the fiscal year. I didn't (and still don't) treat any electronic device as if it were my second heartbeat, and I refused to take work home. My team members were trained, able, and willing to carry on successfully in my absence. But in my mind, I needed to fix every problem because so many people were depending on me! I wanted to make every process better than I found it.

The force behind my work ethic, which may border on workaholic behavior to some, stems from my childhood. I remember the harsh words my grandmother hurled at our mother to make her more dependable. The tone and intent of her words soaked into my spirit at a cellular level. So much so that anything I touch to this day—anything—must be done with the best effort possible. The act of doing anything in a careless manner is unthinkable.

I worked hard to build a career where my name is synonymous with excellence. A subpar effort is never an option! I don't chase perfection, but I also don't bother tracking time when I'm "in the zone." When an issue impacts someone's career, or a problem requires resolution, or someone requests a mentoring session, or I need to create a strategy for a client, time ceases to exist. Each time a team member asked for a records review to better prepare for future opportunities, our session would last for nearly two hours—sometimes longer. My only focus was to inject my talent and tenacity to give others all that's been so graciously given to me—access and opportunity. I will always hold to the Air Force core values of "Service before self" and "Excellence in all we do."

Naturally, my mindset comes at a high cost. I remember attending the retirement ceremony of a colleague who stated the only regret of his career was not making his spouse and children a priority. He stood center stage, receiving accolade upon accolade at one of life's most important milestones—alone. That image never departed my thoughts, but there were times when I—consciously or unconsciously—suppressed the memory. I owe an immeasurable debt to my husband, Andre, and our daughter, Aliyah. Their patience, as I rationalized my way through yet another missed dinner, late arrival, or request to reschedule a function, was monumental. I am eternally grateful that they stood by me, supported me, and challenged me—all the while loving my flawed soul—even when their "love tanks" were running low.

During my long work hours that morphed into months, Team Barnwell maintained without fail our passion for traveling. Each year we took a family vacation for at least a week. No cell phones or computers were allowed. No calls to or from work were permitted, and no paperwork was allowed into my luggage. Aliyah was able to pick a city of her choice to visit each birthday. At the age of 18, the Bank of Mom and Dad amended the by-laws of that agreement (smile). Our trips were always filled with a balance of adventure and leisure to create new memories and reconnect. When I'd begin mapping out a breakneck itinerary, both Andre and Aliyah would give me "the look!" I'd scratch most of the plan to allow for flexibility. Memories of meeting Mickey Mouse or of Aliyah's first rollercoaster ride are magical. The thrill in her eyes as she stood underneath the Eiffel Tower in Paris or trekked across the island of Corfu in Greece on a jeep safari is forever etched in my memory.

I have heartwarming recollections of watching Aliyah and her dad toss a football in the backyard. The look of determination in Aliyah's eyes as she out-maneuvered her dad at indoor Indy car races is unforgettable. The chats at the end of a four-hour Sunday bike ride through German villages will always be extraordinary. Then there's the laughter that erupts to this day when we speak of train rides toward the wrong direction or a packed car so full that we barely made it up the side of a mountain. I'll always treasure the look of awe on Aliyah's face as she watched the King of Blues, Mr. Riley "B.B." King, perform at the North Sea Jazz Festival in Rotterdam on her 12th birthday.

After retiring from the Air Force, I founded and launched an event planning company. An entrepreneurial effort presents its own set of demands, challenges, and rewards for someone with a high intensity, workaholic, or bullet-train mentality. I can honestly say, occasionally traveling at a stagecoach pace isn't a bad thing. Slowing our lives down and being mindful allows us to truly enjoy the greatest aspects of our lives—creating shared experiences with family and friends.

Sincere leaders take care of the team. Leaders are in a place to serve others. We shape futures, motivate, inspire, and, when we lead correctly, become extended family members to those we serve. When asked to cheer someone on during a fitness test, I'd arrive at the track with pom-poms! During award ceremonies, you can count on me to show up with pom-poms and a booming cheer for our honorees. When I promised to attend the graduation ceremony of an Air Force Cadet, I delayed a lucrative business deal to honor my word. During one tour of duty, a young couple had their first child, and our team rallied around them to serve as surrogate family members. Every other month, a little "angel" gave them a small gift for the baby, and a note written in the baby's voice thanking them for their dedication as parents. Those small gestures of joy and thoughtfulness produced lifelong friendships and irreplaceable remembrances.

Good leaders make space for fun. During a particular quarterly awards event, my husband, Andre was an award nominee. While preparing the printed program for the event, a colleague suggested using my favorite "ceremonial" cheer next to his name. Since our team set up the function and created the seating arrangements, we controlled where the "special programs" were placed. When all the people in Andre's civil engineer unit scrolled through their programs, his name was listed as "Master Sergeant Andre 'That's My Baby!' Barnwell." Oh, the look of utter disbelief as he thought of the more than 200 programs containing this phrase—priceless!

Good leaders show dependability by taking care of their bosses. For me, there is a clear distinction between a "boss" and a "toxic leader." Refer to the chapter on integrity for examples. There are several ways to take care of the boss: solve their boss's problems and tell them the truth no matter how challenging the situation. I also think it's essential to exercise a great measure of discretion. When people spend a lot of time together, they learn one another's tendencies, strengths, and shortcomings. Great leaders magnify their boss's positive attributes, balance their flaws, and inform them of any action that lacks diplomacy or appropriateness.

Leaders also demonstrate dependability by managing conflict purposefully and promptly. One of the best ways to lessen the threat of peer negativity is to communicate to everyone you meet your willingness to help every team member make magic. Would you like to take the first step to reduce conflict? Okay, please repeat after me: There is room at the table for every team member. If you have been undermined or sabotaged by a peer, the shock of those actions is gripping. Especially when the person is someone you trusted. For some individuals, the pursuit of power is so great that the damage to another person's reputation is considered insignificant. The person fails to realize that betrayal can have a ripple effect and spread negativity throughout the entire organization. Think about it. How likely are you to trust a fellow team member, coach, supervisor, or manager who spreads malicious and dishonest information?

When I encounter someone spewing lies and who is full of deceit, my initial thought is, "What do they say about me when I'm not present?" No work center is devoid of someone with this behavior. So, here are a few tools that may be helpful. When someone says something you know to be untrue, ask a follow-up question along the lines of, "Do you know that to be true?" If they are repeating something they've heard, they'll have to own it. If they know the statement to be accurate, they'll elaborate (or provide receipts). You may encounter the workplace nosey-rosey. The person begins sizing you up the instant you meet. They'll ask a succession of questions about your professional or personal life. If unchecked, their behavior can become very annoying. Navigate around this person by asking, "What do you plan to do with this information?" Your question will send a signal that they are prying. If the inquiry is appropriate, they will provide a valid explanation for the perceived interrogation.

Lastly, I believe we show dependability as leaders by developing our replacements. You won't be able to serve in your current position forever, so it's essential to cultivate the talent of next-generation leaders. The first day I wore Chief chevrons, I knew every Airman with a capital "A" watched my actions. I gained a renewed commitment to leave the Air Force better than I had found it. I hope you will commit to doing the same as you lead your team.

My desire is for this book to serve as a useful and inspirational leadership tool. May the stories and insight shared influence your behavior to impact the lives of others positively. Use the homework assignments at the end of each chapter to sharpen your leadership skills and develop emerging leaders. Each chapter focuses on behavior to concentrate your efforts on the concept of AIR: action, impact, and result. I am sure you will heighten awareness, confidence, expertise, knowledge, ingenuity, talent, and skills for yourself and others. Continue to prepare people to achieve their next big thing and in doing so, help the team soar!

"The most precious gift we can offer anyone is our attention."

- Thich Nhat Hanh,
Spiritual Leader, Poet, and Activist

Chapter 9 Homework: Dependable

#Recall | How do you practice dependability with:

Yourself

_____

_____

Your family

_____

_____

Your team

_____

_____

Your peers

_____

_____

Your boss

_____

_____

What areas can you improve?

_____

_____

_____

_____

_____

#Relate | Have you experienced sabotage by a coworker?

_____

_____

How did the experience make you feel?

_____

_____

How did you respond?

_____

_____

Have you undermined or sabotaged a colleague, team member, team lead, or supervisor?

_____

_____

What was the rationale for your action?

_____

_____

_____

What did you hope to gain/achieve from your action?

_____

_____

_____

_____

_____

_____

_____

#Act | What actions are you taking to make your company, organization, or agency a better place once you transition to your next big thing?

_____

_____

_____

_____

_____

_____

_____

_____

_____

_____

_____

_____

_____

_____

_____

_____

_____

_____

_____

Recap

All military training and learning platforms follow three protocols: tell the audience what they will learn, give the audience the message, and finally, remind the audience of the message shared. This recap briefly highlights the themes and concepts presented in the book. The activities and prompts help boost awareness and application.

I chose to name this book *Leadership Is About Behavior, Not Titles,* because at the heart of being an effective leader is the willingness to create and maintain healthy relationships. Our behavior determines every measure of success—or failure within our teams, family life, and personal growth.

Whether you are a new team member, a front-line supervisor, or a senior executive, your commitment to caring for people cannot be overstated. The foundation of building a healthy relationship begins with showing others respect. As we provide support, offer cooperation, cultivate trust, remain honest, and stay accountable, we position ourselves to connect with others in a wholesome way. When we drop our guards and show vulnerabilities and fears, we signal to those around us that the space we share is safe—a place were everyone can grow.

Again, I offer my most impactful leadership advice:

#1 – Be a voice for the voiceless.

#2 – Be fair and consistent in all matters.

#3 – Surround yourself with good people.

#4 – Don't ask people to do something you wouldn't do.

Character—The mental and moral qualities distinctive to an individual; a person's good reputation.

Who are you when no one is watching? Who are you when everyone is watching? In the face of adversity, stress, and deadlines, we may come 'out of character' to deal with challenges. Our ultimate goal is to be deeply rooted in fairness, so difficulties rarely shake our foundation of goodness and strength. Great leaders do the right thing, no matter the sacrifice or consequence.

"The only true regrets in life come from inaction."

- Dr. John W. Carlos, Olympian and Activist

Use the word **character** to make five new words:

Example: Heart

1.

2.

3.

4.

5.

I will safeguard my character by

_____

_____

_____

_____

_____

Courage—The ability to do something that is frightening; strength in the face of pain or grief.

You have a hard decision to make. One option pleases your team, and the other choice would satisfy management. Which direction will you go? In moments like these, courage is vital. Instances such as these can expose our vulnerabilities. Are you courageous enough to seek advice from experienced leaders? Are you willing to admit your lack of knowledge on the topic and request more information? If time permits, are you comfortable asking for a deadline extension to better access impacts? Good leaders are truthful and fearless.

"Courage starts with showing up and letting ourselves be seen."

- Dr. Brené Brown, Professor and Author

Use the word **courage** to make three new words:

Example: Grace

1.

2.

3.

4.

5.

I will display courage by

_____

_____

_____

Optimistic— Hopeful and confident about the future.

You have a colleague who rarely shares a positive thought or perspective. Each encounter with this person is filled with complaints about fellow team members, the work center, management, assigned projects, new policies, or today's weather. In their view of life, nothing is ever right. Now, you can adopt the same beliefs, or you can focus on how to create change. Of course, you can't change the weather, but you can adjust your perspective. When I was stationed in Germany, the locals quickly reminded Americans that there's no such thing as bad weather, only bad clothing. Respected leaders find solutions, are mindful, and promote harmony.

"Optimistic, hopeful people view barriers and obstacles as problems to be solved and not as the reason to give up or turn back. Positive people never, ever give up."

- Wilma Mankiller, Principal Chief of the
Cherokee Nation and Activist

When faced with obstacles, I will remain optimistic by

_____

_____

_____

_____

_____

_____

Leadership—the action of leading a group of people or an organization.

Leaders have the opportunity to reshape the life and careers of others **and** a responsibility to do so. When you back your team's decisions, serve as a mentor, or agree to collaborate with a colleague on a major objective or goal, you reinforce respected leadership behavior. Esteemed leaders consistently develop next-generation leaders.

"True leadership stems from individuality that is honestly and sometimes imperfectly expressed ... Leaders should strive for authenticity over perfection."

- Sheryl Sandberg, Chief Operating Officer of Facebook

I will demonstrate leadership by

_____

_____

_____

_____

_____

_____

_____

_____

_____

_____

_____

```
C   H   A   R   A   C   T   E   R   V   C   I
Y   E   E   Z   A   N   Q   U   B   I   T   N
I   V   M   G   F   C   D   H   T   L   R   T
M   X   I   P   A   M   T   S   N   E   O   E
P   Z   W   S   C   R   I   I   M   N   P   G
A   Y   D   O   I   M   U   O   O   S   P   R
C   Z   A   N   I   O   T   O   T   N   U   I
T   C   F   T   U   I   N   L   C   G   S   T
H   N   P   C   O   X   U   A   V   D   J   Y
U   O   F   N   W   S   D   I   R   E   C   T
E   T   A   G   E   L   E   D   M   Y   P   I
G   L   R   R   J   J   M   R   A   O   S   C
```

Find and Circle

Five leadership traits	♫ ♫ ♫ ♫ ♫
Four basic leadership styles	♫ ♫ ♫ ♫
Three words defining AIR	♫ ♫ ♫
One type of empathy	♫
A leader helps others	♫

Puzzle solutions:

Five leadership traits

   - character, courage, optimistic, visionary, integrity

Four basic leadership styles

   - direct, coach, support, delegate

Three words defining AIR

   - action, impact, results

One type of empathy

   - emotional

A leader helps others

   - soar

Emotional Intelligence—the capacity to be aware of, control, and express one's emotions, and to handle interpersonal relationships judiciously and empathetically.

As a leader, how do you express disappointment to your team? Are you treating *each* team member fairly? Do you listen with a third ear? What actions have you taken to tame the office bully? How are you managing your urge to micromanage? Phenomenal leaders illustrate emotional intelligence by listening and acknowledging the viewpoints of others. Leaders also ensure the trust factor is never broken.

"Think of the person you most respect and approach everyone you lead with the same measure of respect and disposition."

- Shon Barnwell, Veteran and Author

Use **emotional intelligence** to make five new words:

Example: *Inclination*

1.

2.

3.

4.

5.

I will express emotional intelligence by

_____

_____

_____

Visionary—thinking about or planning the future with imagination or wisdom.

It is said that if you are the smartest person in the room, you're in the wrong room! Mature leaders surround themselves with superb talent. They strategically push team members to achieve new levels of fulfillment by stepping out of their comfort zones. Distinguished leaders ask, "What would you do if you knew you could not fail?"

**"Don't be afraid to go out on a limb.
That's where the fruit is."**

- H. Jackson Browne Jr., Author

Use the word **visionary** to make five new words:

Example: *Soar*

1.

2.

3.

4.

5.

I will exhibit visionary leadership by

_____

_____

_____

_____

_____

nspirational—providing or showing creative or spiritual inspiration.

In every leadership role, you will encounter people who meet one of three criteria: willing, capable, or unable to achieve a task. Your first responsibility is to assess each team member and determine their level of motivation, skills, and aptitude. Afterward, you begin leveraging your talent to influence and inspire continued success or improved performance. When leaders show genuine concern, the people around them will go above and beyond to reach the desired expectation or goal.

"How can I go out there and create value?"

- Stedman Graham, Educator and Author

Use the word **inspirational** to make five new words:

Example: *Liaison*

1.

2.

3.

4.

5.

I will embody inspirational leadership by

_____

_____

_____

Effective Communicator—a person who is able to convey or exchange information, news, or ideas, in an eloquent or skilled manner.

All leaders must ensure they develop effective communication skills. The platform used to share information is determined by the urgency of the message. How a leader speaks to others is paramount to conveying respect. Putting data into the proper context so all team members can grasp details and act is also essential. Lastly, respected leaders know that sharing information builds trust and allows teams to be responsive and proactive.

Unscramble each of the clue words below.

AEMT   ___   ___   ___   ___
             *   *   *   *

COIVE   ___   ___   ___   ___   ___
             *   *   *

TNEO   ___   ___   ___   ___
             *

Take the letters that appear with the * beneath them and unscramble them for the final message. _____

I will practice **effective communication** by

_____

_____

ntegrity—the quality of being honest and having strong moral principles.

The spirit of an organization's climate and culture is in jeopardy when a leader lacks integrity. Leaders who do not treat others with respect or fail to keep their promises will quickly erode a team's health. When a team operates from a position of fear and distrust, many negative behaviors can surface. The resulting actions can be lost talent, high turnover, stressful working environments, shattered morale, and infighting. Celebrated leaders know they must set the example in their behavior for others to follow.

Use the word **integrity** to make five new words:

Example: Ignite

1.

2.

3.

4.

5.

I will personify integrity by

_____

_____

_____

_____

_____

_____

_____

Puzzle Solutions:

Unscramble each of the clue words below.

AEMT   T   E   A   M
           *   *   *   *

COIVE   V   O   I   C   E
           *   *   *

TNEO   T   O   N   E
           *

Take the letters that appear with the * beneath them and unscramble them for the final message. **<u>MOTIVATE</u>**

Dependable—trustworthy and reliable.

Who's depending on you right now? Who did you give your word to and failed to deliver on your promise? What actions do you take to resolve conflict, so everyone wins? How do you support diversity, inclusion, and equality? When was the last time you scanned the work climate for non-conforming behaviors? Well-regarded leaders understand the value trust plays in team cohesion, and they protect it at all costs. Every leader must work to leave their post or position better than they found it.

I will prove myself dependable by

_____

_____

_____

_____

_____

_____

_____

_____

_____

_____

_____

_____

_____

The Airman's Creed

I am an American Airman.
I am a Warrior.
I have answered my nation's call.

I am an American Airman.
My mission is to fly, fight, and win.
I am faithful to a proud heritage,
a tradition of honor,
and a legacy of valor.

I am an American Airman.
Guardian of freedom and justice,
My nation's sword and shield,
Its sentry and avenger.
I defend my country with my life.
I am an American Airman:
Wingman, Leader, Warrior.

I will never leave an Airman behind.
I will never falter,
and I will not fail.

The Optimist's Creed

by Christian D. Larson

Promise Yourself

To be so strong that nothing can disturb your peace of mind.

To talk health, happiness and prosperity to every person you meet.

To make all your friends feel that there is something in them.

To look at the sunny side of everything and make your optimism come true.

To think only of the best, to work only for the best, and to expect only the best.

To be just as enthusiastic about the success of others as you are about your own.

To forget the mistakes of the past and press on to the greater achievements of the future.

To wear a cheerful countenance at all times and give every living creature you meet a smile.

To give so much time to the improvement of yourself that you have no time to criticize others.

To be too large for worry, too noble for anger, too strong for fear, and too happy to permit the presence of trouble.

Desiderata

by Max Ehrmann

Go placidly amid the noise and haste, and remember what peace there may be in silence. As far as possible without surrender be on good terms with all persons. Speak your truth quietly and clearly; and listen to others, even the dull and the ignorant; they too have their story. Avoid loud and aggressive persons, they are vexations to the spirit. If you compare yourself with others, you may become vain and bitter; for always there will be greater and lesser persons than yourself. Enjoy your achievements as well as your plans. Keep interested in your own career, however humble; it is a real possession in the changing fortunes of time. Exercise caution in your business affairs; for the world is full of trickery. But let this not blind you to what virtue there is; many persons strive for high ideals; and everywhere life is full of heroism. Be yourself. Especially, do not feign affection. Neither be cynical about love; for in the face of aridity and disenchantment it is as perennial as the grass. Take kindly the counsel of the years, gracefully surrendering the things of youth. Nurture strength of spirit to shield you in sudden misfortune. But do not distress yourself with dark imaginings. Many fears are born of fatigue and loneliness. Beyond a wholesome discipline, be gentle with yourself. You are a child of the universe, no less than the trees and the stars; you have a right to be here. And whether or not it is clear to you, no doubt the universe is unfolding as it should. Therefore be at peace with God, whatever you conceive Him to be, and whatever your labors and aspirations, in the noisy confusion of life keep peace with your soul. With all its sham, drudgery, and broken dreams, it is still a beautiful world. Be cheerful. Strive to be happy.

Afterword

Yes, leading others is a challenging and sometimes frustrating effort. But it's likely to be one of your most rewarding life experiences as well. Don't be afraid to take the first step to build your skills! I believe everyone has a superpower. My greatest joy is helping people realize and achieve their goals. The nine leadership behaviors presented in this book serve as my beacon to inspire you. I hope you embrace the traits as you provide your team with world-class dedication, unfaltering respect and honesty, and remarkable authenticity.

Everything you touch #MakeMagic

Every challenge you face #KeepSoaring

Every team you lead #BuildAIR

Every dream you hold #GoGetIt

Every day you awaken #CreateTheSpace

#MamaShonOut

Learn More

Thank you for the graciousness of your time! I appreciate you reading this book. My sincerest desire is to share insight to help you create the space to expand your leadership tool kit. I also want you to perform at your most tremendous potential. May this book encourage all leaders to authentically care for every member of their team!

This book is an excellent resource for professional development programs, mentoring sessions, roundtable discussions, workshops, professional reading lists, book clubs, growth and development initiatives, and emerging leader training, to name a few applications.

Share your thoughts at:

Twitter: @BarnwellPublish
Facebook: @BarnwellPublishing
Email: BarnwellPublishing@gmail.com
Website: www.BarnwellPublishing.com

Invite me to host an impactful workshop for your team or speak at an event! I am very passionate about taking care of people and helping others lead with AIR: action, impact, and result. Reach me at **BarnwellPublishing@gmail.com.**

About the Author

Shon Barnwell served in the United States Air Force for 25 years, reshaping organizations on five continents. Her areas of expertise include project management, logistics, process improvement, on-demand training, and consulting. She served in numerous leadership positions at the squadron, group, wing, numbered Air Force, and major command levels. Shon deployed in support of Operation Southern Watch in Bahrain, Operation Iraqi Freedom in Iraq, and Operation Enduring Freedom in Afghanistan. As a Superintendent, she was responsible for all matters affecting morale, welfare, resiliency, retention, recruitment, and readiness of more than 71,000 service members. Shon rose to the rank of Chief

Master Sergeant—a rank that reflects only 1% of the enlisted force. She retired honorably from the Air Force in 2014.

After retiring, Shon started an event planning company to provide professional, engaging, and memorable experiences for clients and their guests. She has launched 215+ successful conferences, workshops, and special events, managed a budget of $3.5 million, and delighted more 35,000 people. In 2018, the National Veteran-Owned Business Association (NaVOBA) selected her company as a Minority

Business Enterprise of the Year finalist. She leverages her travels to 26 countries to provide premier hospitality services. Shon conducts impactful workshops on leadership, conflict management, team building, inclusion and diversity, and business etiquette for professionals and emerging leaders.

Her entrepreneurial efforts include:

- National Center for Veteran Institute for Procurement (VIP) START, Maryland Chamber

- University of Connecticut's In-Residence Entrepreneurship Bootcamp for Veterans (EBV) with Disabilities

- 2 x VetSmallBiz Challenge Finalist, Institute for Veterans and Military Families (IVMF)

- Veteran Women Igniting the Spirit of Entrepreneurship (V-WISE), Charlotte, NC

- City of Warner Robins Independence Day Celebration, GA

- Black Enterprise Women of Power Summit, Phoenix, AZ

- V-WISE Inaugural IGNITE Program, Savannah, GA

- Daymond John's Success Formula Entrepreneurial Training

- Sandler Sales Training, Alpharetta, GA

- Launched Barnwell Publishing, LLC

Shon is a Doctor of Business Administration (DBA) Candidate at Trident International University. She previously served as a board member for the Robins Regional Chamber of

Commerce, Family Promise of Greater Houston County, and Delta Mu Delta Lambda Sigma Virtual Co-Chapter. Shon currently serves as a board member for the Warner Robins Convention and Visitors Bureau. She is also a Houston County High School Business and Computer Science advisory council member. Shon serves as a mentor to veteran entrepreneurs and speaks on entrepreneurial and leadership topics. She resides in Warner Robins, Georgia, with her husband, Master Sergeant Andre Barnwell, USAF, Retired; and their daughter, Aliyah.

"Don't judge each day by the harvest you reap but by the seeds that you plant."

- Robert Louis Stevenson

#LetsGo #CreateTheSpace #ChangeTheWorld